P9-ELR-089

Quick Tricks for Holidays

by Annalisa McMorrow
illustrated by Marilynn G. Barr

This book is for Devon. She makes every day a holiday.

Publisher: Roberta Suid
Design & Production: Standing Watch Productions
Cover Design: David Hale

Entire contents copyright © 2001 by
Monday Morning Books, Inc.
For a complete catalog, please write to the address below:

Monday Morning Books
P.O. Box 1680
Palo Alto, CA 94302

E-mail us at: MMBooks@aol.com
Visit our Web site: www.mondaymorningbooks.com
Call us at: 1-800-255-6049

Monday Morning is a registered trademark of
Monday Morning Books, Inc.

Permission is hereby granted to reproduce student materials
in this book for non-commercial individual or classroom use.

ISBN 1-57612-141-0

Printed in the United States of America
987654321

Contents

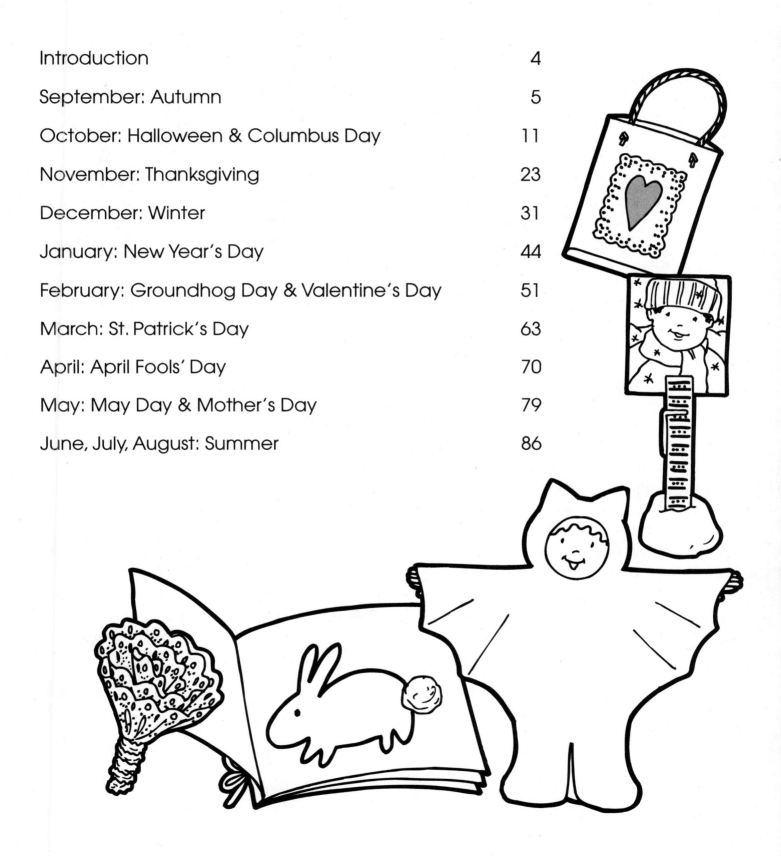

INTRODUCTION

Being a teacher is time consuming. That's why the activities in *Quick Tricks for Holidays* are easy to do. Most of the projects require six or fewer items on the materials list and the majority have only a few steps. Even more important, all are fun!

For added flexibility, some activities can be used for more than one holiday if you make simple changes. For instance, several Valentine's Day cards would work for Mother's Day, Father's Day, or winter holidays simply by changing the shape of the decorations. (Instead of a foil heart, children might make a foil snowflake. Instead of painting with red Jell-O for Valentine's Day, children can paint with lime green Jell-O for St. Patrick's Day.)

Many basic holidays are featured, including Halloween, Thanksgiving, New Year's Day, St. Patrick's Day, Earth Day, and the Fourth of July. Also included are seasonal celebrations for autumn, winter, spring, and summer. These ideas are meant to help you and your students have fun with the changing of the year. It's a way to look at every day as a celebration!

Each section of the book begins with a poem. Read the poems to the children, then post them on a bulletin board in the classroom. (Consider adding color to the borders around the poems.) You might even send the poems home with the children to share with their families.

Included in the chapters are ideas for cards to exchange, games to play, gifts to make, puppets to use in dramatic play, and more. Each chapter also includes one page of patterns. These can be used with many of the activities or enlarged and displayed in the classroom as seasonal or holiday decorations. Use your creativity with the patterns—some will make good cubby labels or name tags to be worn on field trips. Others work well as borders for bulletin boards.

Further enhance these holiday activities by making a book link, playing festive music, or serving holiday-themed snacks. Some suggestions are included here. . . but use them as a springboard for your own creative ideas!

Have fun, and happy holidays!

September: Autumn

The sunshine's happy rays,
Warm summer's golden days.
But soon the summer's done.
And autumn has begun.

The leaves turn gold and red,
And fall upon your head,
Then crinkle on the ground
And make a crunchy sound.

It's time for hats and coats,
A scarf around your throat,
Under umbrellas huddle,
And skip through autumn's puddles.

The squirrels scurry around,
To pick nuts off the ground,
And store them all away,
For a winter's day.

Darkness creeps up soon.
With autumn's harvest moon.
It shines down on us all.
There's beauty in the fall!

Name Plates
A Quick Trick with Twigs and Sticks

Children can use these name plates to mark their cubbies, or they can bring them home to hang from their bedroom doors.

Materials:
Index cards
Glue
Twigs and sticks
Crayons or markers
Hole punch
Yarn or ribbon

Directions:
1. Write each child's name on an index card.
2. Take the children for a nature walk to collect fall items: small twigs, leaves, acorns, and so on.
3. Have the children decorate their name cards by gluing on the fall items.
4. Punch two holes in the cards and thread through with a piece of colorful yarn or ribbon for easy hanging.

Option:
• Duplicate the Autumn Patterns (p. 7) for use instead of real items from nature.

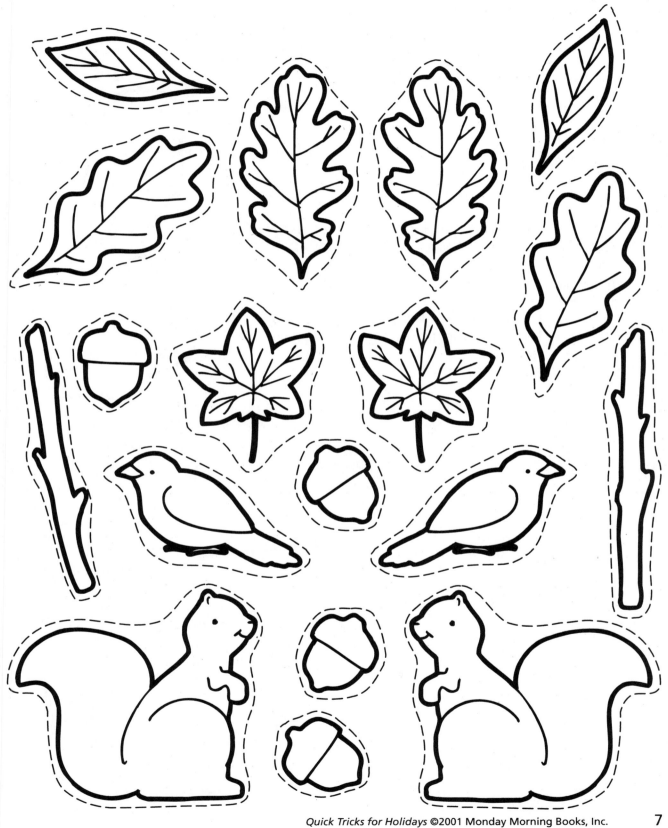

Sponge-Printed Pictures
A Quick Trick with Sponges

These autumn-themed pictures are a perfect way to introduce the children to each other.

Materials:
Sponges
Scissors
Tempera paint
Shallow tins for paint
Paper

Directions:
1. Cut the sponges into autumn shapes such as leaves. (You can use the Autumn Patterns as templates to cut out pictures from the sponges.)
2. Have the children use the sponges to create printed pictures. Provide tempera paint in various fall colors for this activity.
3. Once the pictures have dried, have the children give their pictures a name. They can then introduce themselves and their pictures to the class.
4. Post the pictures in an autumn-themed display.

Options:
• Invite other classes in to see your gallery of autumn pictures.
• Children can further decorate their pictures with crayons, markers, or items glued to the paper.

A squirrel is in the leaves.

Toss the Nuts to the Squirrel
A Quick Trick with Beanbags

This fun bean-bag game gives the children a chance
to test their tossing skills.

Materials:
Beanbags
Basket
Large sheet of poster board
Marker

Directions:
1. Draw a squirrel on the sheet of poster board.
2. Place the basket on the floor in front of the squirrel.
3. Tell the children that they will be pretending the beanbags
are acorns.
4. Have the children take turns tossing the "acorn" beanbags
into the basket.

Option:
• Enlarge the squirrel from the Autumn Patterns (p. 7) and glue
it to the board.

Fall Wreath
A Quick Trick with a Paper Plate

Hang these wreaths in the classroom, or let the children take them home to hang on their walls.

Materials:
Paper plates (one per child)
Glue
Tissue paper in autumn colors (gold, red, orange, brown)
Scissors (for adult use only)
Yarn

Directions:
1. Cut a circle in the middle of each paper plate. (To do this, you might need to gently fold the plates in half.) Make one wreath for each child.
2. Have the children tear the tissue paper into scraps and then glue the scraps to the wreaths.
3. Help the children to tie a piece of yarn through the center of the wreath to hang from a door.

Options:
• Have the children gather assorted items from nature to glue to their wreaths—they might use leaves, twigs, flower petals, or acorns.
• Duplicate the Autumn Patterns (p. 7) for the children to glue to their wreaths.

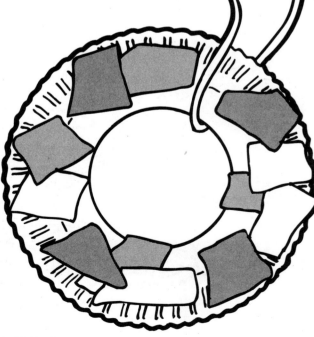

October: Halloween

Halloween's the time of year
To choose with care the things you wear.

You want to look your very best,
But still stand out from all the rest.

Will you dress as a ghost or cat,
A dog, a pirate, or a bat?

A monster, maybe, something scary,
Or a teddy bear that's hairy.

Put on your costume, choose your clothes,
If you're a clown, wear a red nose!

The time is right to have a meeting
With your friends for trick-or-treating.

But since it's dark, please do what's right,
When you go out, bring your flashlight!

Nina, Pinta, Santa Maria
A Quick Trick with Milk Cartons

Use these simple boats in a Christopher Columbus display.

Materials:
Milk cartons (one for every two children)
Scissors or craft knife (for adult use only)
Construction paper scraps
Glue
Books about Christopher Columbus
Marker

Directions:
1. Cut the cartons in half lengthwise to create two boat shapes.
2. Give each child a boat to decorate using paper scraps and glue.
3. Help the children name their boats either the Nina, Pinta, or Santa Maria.
4. Display the boats near books about Christopher Columbus and Columbus Day.

Options:
• Provide plastic toy people to stand in the boats.
• Keep several boats free of decorations for use in the water table.

Book Links:
• *Christopher Columbus: Step Into Reading* by Stephen Krensky (Random House, 1991).
• *Christopher Columbus Paper Dolls in Full Color* by Tom Tierney (Dover, 1992).
• *Columbus Day: Let's Meet Christopher Columbus* by Barbara de Rubertis (Kane, 1996).

Painted Paper Bag Pumpkins
A Quick Trick with a Lunch Bag

Decorate the classroom with this festive Halloween display.

Materials:
Paper bags (lunch-bag size, one per child)
Tempera paint
Paintbrushes
Newspaper
Green ribbon
Green construction paper
Scissors
Glue

Directions:
1. Have the children stuff the paper bags with crumpled newspaper.
2. Tie the tops closed with green ribbon.
3. Provide tempera paint for the children to use to paint their pumpkins. They can mix the paints to make orange.
4. Once the paper bags have dried, the children can paint faces on their pumpkins.
5. Children can cut leaves from the green construction paper to glue to the top of their paper pumpkins.

Option:
• Display the pumpkins on a shelf in the classroom. Add straw, dried ears of corn, dried leaves, or other fall items.

Candy-Holding Bags
A Quick Trick with a Paper Bag

Children can use this decorated bag to gather goodies on Halloween.

Materials:
Paper bags (one per child)
Drawing paper
Crayons
Scissors
Glitter
Glue
Squeeze bottles

Directions:
1. Have the children draw pictures of items that represent Halloween to them—for instance, children in costumes, jack-o'lanterns, candy, or black cats.
2. Have the children cut out their pictures and glue them to the paper bags.
3. Children can add designs on their bags using glitter mixed with glue in squeeze bottles.
4. Let the bags dry before sending them home with the children.

Options:
• Children can cut out pictures from magazines to glue to their bags.
• Bags of a variety of sizes would work with this activity. However, bags with handles are especially useful.
• Use this activity as a way to decorate gift bags for other holidays. (Children could draw other pictures, such as snowflakes, presents, or snowmen.)

Simple Ghosty
A Quick Trick with a Pillowcase

This little ghosty can dress up a pillow with Halloween spirit. Or it can be used to carry loot on Halloween night.

Materials:
White pillowcases (one per child)
Black felt
Glue
Scissors (for adult use only)

Directions:
1. Cut circles from the felt. Make two per child.
2. Have the children place their pillowcases flat on a table.
3. Each child should glue two circular eyes to a pillowcase.

Option:
• White pillowcases make the most standard-looking ghosts, but other colors can become different creatures. For instance, children can make black cats from black pillowcases, gluing on triangular ears, green oval eyes, and little pink noses.

Envelope Halloween Puppet
A Quick Trick with an Envelope

These may be the very easiest puppets to make.

Materials:
White letter-sized envelopes (one per child)
Scissors
Crayons

Directions:
1. Give each child an envelope.
2. Have the children seal the envelopes.
3. Demonstrate how to draw a ghost lengthwise on the envelope. It can simply be a flat-bottomed oval with two circular eyes.
4. Help children cut the bottom edges from the envelopes.
5. The children can put their ghost puppets on their hands and stage Halloween puppet shows.

Option:
• Duplicate the Halloween Patterns (p. 17) for children to cut out, color, and glue to envelopes to make puppets.

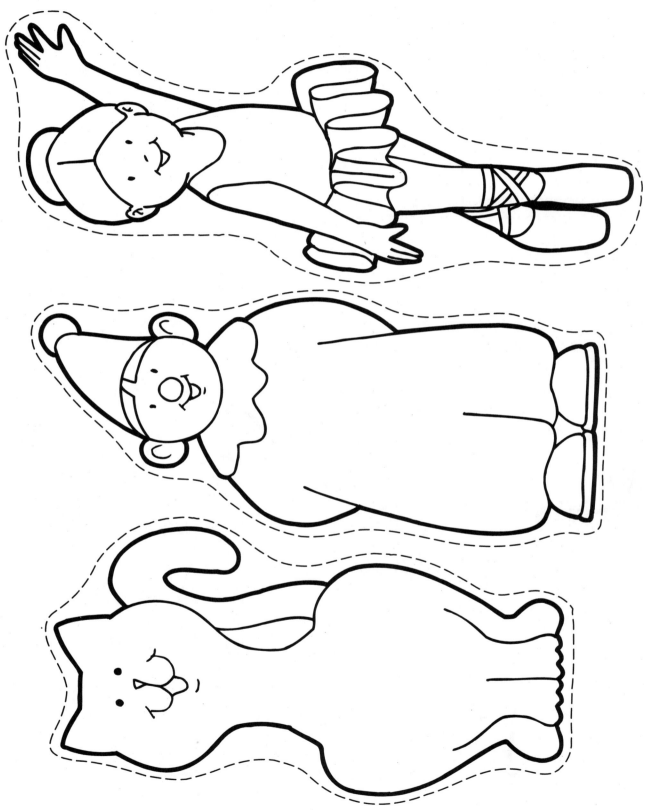

Scary Sweets
A Quick Trick with a Tissue

These ghostly lollipops can be given as gifts or enjoyed by the children.

Materials:
Lollipops (one per child)
White tissues (one per child)
Ribbon
Nontoxic black markers

Directions:
1. Give each child a lollipop.
2. Demonstrate how to cover the lollipop with the tissue.
3. Help the children tie a ribbon around the neck of the lollipop to fasten the tissue to the stick.
4. Have the children draw two eyes on their covered lollipops to create a ghost.

Option:
• Instead of lollipops, use round balls of clay stuck to the end of craft sticks.

Quick Tricks for Holidays ©2001 Monday Morning Books, Inc.

Jack-o'-Orange
A Quick Trick with Oranges

These miniature jack-o'-lanterns are much easier to create than ones carved from pumpkins.

Materials:
Oranges (one per child)
Whole cloves

Directions:
1. Demonstrate how to create these little jack-o'-oranges. Use the cloves to make a face on the orange.
2. Give each child an orange and a handful of cloves. The children will stick the cloves into the oranges to make Halloween faces.
3. Display the jack-o'-oranges, or let the children take them home. After Halloween, the oranges can be eaten.

Option:
• Children can draw faces on the oranges rather than use cloves.
• Create other Halloween displays by letting the children draw faces on miniature pumpkins rather than carve the pumpkins.

Puppet Ghosts
A Quick Trick with Paper Plates

Two paper plates can easily become ghost hand puppets.

Materials:
Paper plates (two per child)
Black crayons
Scissors (for adult use only)
Tape or glue

Directions:
1. Have the children tape or glue the plates together so that the top edges are aligned.
2. The children can each decorate one side of the taped plates to look like a ghost's face.
3. Cut the bottom from the plates so that a child can insert his or her hand into the opening.
4. Children can work their puppets to various Halloween songs and rhymes, such as the one on the next page. (This is a counting rhyme and five children can work as a team to act out the parts.)

Option:
• Send the poem home with the children. They can share it with their families.

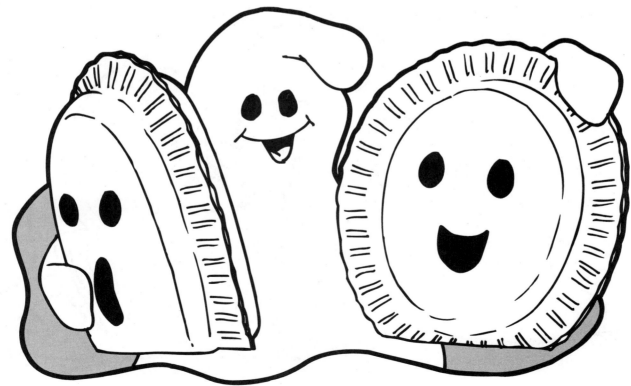

Quick Tricks for Holidays ©2001 Monday Morning Books, Inc.

Five Friendly Ghosts

On Halloween, you just might see,
Five friendly ghosts up in a tree.

If one ghost wants to fly away,
Four little ghosts will jump and play.

If one more ghost decides to flee,
The number of ghosts will be three.

If one more leaves, there will be two
Nice friendly ghosts left to say, "Boo!"

If one more ghost leaves all the fun,
Then left behind there will be one.

And if that ghost then takes a fright,
No ghosts will stay Halloween Night!

Funny Masks
A Quick Trick with Paper Plates

Children can use these masks on Halloween in the classroom.

Materials:
Paper plates (one per child)
Scissors (for adult use only)
Plastic spoons (one per child)
Crayons or markers
Decorations (tissue paper, construction paper, feathers, glitter, sequins, felt scraps, and so on)
Glue
Heavy-duty packing tape

Directions:
1. Help each child to create a mask by holding a plate to a child's face and marking where the eyes and mouth are. Cut out eye holes and a mouth hole for the children.
2. Have the children decide what they want their masks to look like. Stage a brainstorming session if children need help. They might create clown masks, scary masks, jack-o'-lantern masks, silly masks, and so on.
3. Provide assorted materials for the children to use to decorate their masks.
4. Children glue a spoon to the back of their masks for the handle. Reinforce this handle with a strip of heavy-duty packing tape.

Option:
• Host a masquerade "ball" in which the children hide behind their masks and dare their friends to guess who they are.

Quick Tricks for Holidays ©2001 Monday Morning Books, Inc.

November: Thanksgiving

Thanksgiving is a time to munch
On a very festive lunch.

Eat some brussels sprouts and ham,
Turkey, stuffing, and some yams.

If you can, save room for sweets,
Pumpkin. pie and other treats.

But Thanksgiving's more than food,
Happiness fills people's moods.

So give thanks for all you see—
That is, unless you're a turkey!

Leaf-Rubbing Wreath
A Quick Trick with Autumn Leaves

This colorful wreath can decorate your classroom door.

Materials:
Leaves (one per child)
Crayons or markers
Scissors (for adult use only)
Drawing paper
Paper plate
Glue

Directions:
1. Have each child bring a leaf to school.
2. Show the children how to make rubbings of their leaves.
3. Help the children to cut out the rubbings.
4. Cut a hole in the center of the paper plate.
5. Glue the leaf rubbings all around the rim of the paper plate in a ring. The leaves should completely cover the plate.
6. Post the finished wreath on your door.

Options:
• Write each child's name on his or her rubbing.
• Help identify the different leaves brought in to the classroom.
• Go on a nature walk to gather the leaves.
• Use the leaves in the activity "Turkey Centerpiece" (p. 25).

Turkey Centerpiece
Another Quick Trick with Autumn Leaves

Set the perfect Thanksgiving table with this cute centerpiece in the middle.

Materials:
Leaves (several per child)
Small paper plates (one per child)
Glue
Crayons or markers

Directions:
1. Give each child a paper plate. Have the children decorate it to look like a turkey's face.
2. Have the children glue the leaves to the back of the plate so that the leaves appear like feathers behind the turkey.

Options:
• Children can draw turkeys on construction paper and glue on the leaf-feathers.
• Make one turkey for the class. Each child brings in a leaf to glue to a large class turkey that the teacher creates.
• Use the Turkey Pattern for the children. They can color the turkey and glue leaves to the back.

Turkey Pattern

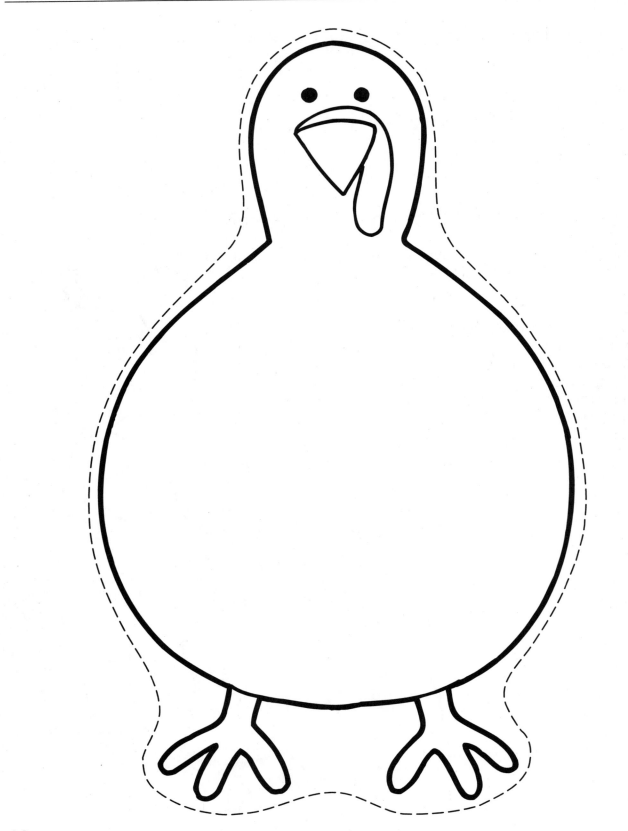

 Quick Tricks for Holidays ©2001 Monday Morning Books, Inc.

Holiday Meal Place Cards
A Quick Trick with the Sunday Funnies

Help holiday guests find their places easily with these silly place cards.

Materials:
Index cards
Crayons or markers
Glue
Scissors
Funnies from the Sunday paper

Directions:
1. For each place card, the children will fold an index card in half.
2. Have the children cut out pictures they like from the comics.
3. The children can glue their pictures to the place cards.
4. Help the children write their names on their cards.
5. Children can make extra cards to bring home for adults in the family to use by adding the names of guests.

Option:
• Use comics from the daily paper and let children color the black-and-white pictures with crayons.

Napkin Rings
A Quick Trick with Paper Towel Tubes

These colorful napkin holders make perfect holiday presents for the children to give to their families.

Materials:
Paper towel tubes (one for every two children)
Scissors (for adult use only)
Tempera paint
Paintbrushes
Ribbon
Sequins or glitter and glue (optional)

Directions:
1. Cut each paper towel tube into eight sections. Give each child four.
2. Have the children decorate the sections using tempera paint. They can add sparkle to the dried sections with sequins or glitter and glue.
3. Once the napkin rings have dried, tie them together in bunches using ribbon.
4. The children can take their napkin rings home to their families.

Options:
• Make the glue sparkle by mixing the glitter into it ahead of time.
• Children can decorate the rings with drawings to celebrate specific holidays—a turkey for Thanksgiving, snowflakes or snowmen for any winter holiday, hearts for Valentine's Day, and so on.

Rebus Menus
A Quick Trick with the Grocery Ads

Children will make picture menus to accompany their
Thanksgiving meals.

Materials:
Grocery ads from the Sunday paper (these are usually in color)
Heavy paper
Scissors
Glue

Directions:
1. Have the children cut out pictures of different types of foods
served at their house on Thanksgiving. Help children who need
extra assistance.
2. Give each child a piece of heavy paper.
3. Have the children glue the pictures to the paper to make rebus
menus. These can be sent home with them for use as displays on
the Thanksgiving table.

Option:
• Ahead of time, brainstorm with the students the types of food
served on Thanksgiving. The children can then look for these foods
in the ads.

Thanksgiving Turkey Puppets
A Quick Trick with Craft Sticks

Children can make these puppets very quickly.

Materials:
Craft sticks
Feathers
Googly eyes
Glue
Crayons and markers

Directions:
1. Give each child five craft sticks.
2. Provide feathers, googly eyes, and crayons and markers for the children to use to make simple turkeys. The children glue eyes to the front of the craft sticks and feathers to the rear.
3. Have the children use the puppets while you read the poem below. (It's a retelling of the Five Friendly Ghosts rhyme from Halloween.)

Option:
• Duplicate the Turkey Pattern (p. 26) for children to color, cut out, and glue to craft sticks.

Five Little Turkeys
On Thanksgiving, you just might see,
Five little turkeys in a tree.
If one little turkey flies away,
Four little turkeys now will play.
If one more turkey has to flee,
The turkeys left will number three.
If one more turkey flaps his wings,
Two turkeys will be left to sing.
If another leaves the fun,
Then left behind there will be one.
And if that turkey then takes flight,
We won't have turkey Thanksgiving night!

December: Winter

Snowflakes, snowflakes galore.
Snowflakes, snowflakes, and more.

See them dancing in air.
Fluttering everywhere.

Watch them land on the trees.
Coating branches and leaves.

The world looks like a dream.
Coated with snow-like cream.

Just like friends who you know,
People are quite like snow.

If you think that it's right,
No snowflakes are alike.

Snowflakes, snowflakes, and more.
Snowflakes, snowflakes galore.

Pipe Cleaner Candy Canes
A Quick Trick with Pipe Cleaners

You can hang these colorful candy canes around the classroom.

Materials:
Pipe cleaners in a variety of colors

Directions:
1. To make each candy cane, have the children take two pipe cleaners that are different colors and twist them together. The two pipe cleaners will form one column that is a spiral of two colors.
2. The children bend over one end of the column to make a candy cane shape.
3. Let the children make many different candy canes. They can make the usual white and red ones or create a variety of colorful canes. These decorations can be hung from a tree or from a clothesline strung across the room.

Option:
• Have the children glue small magnets to their canes to make holiday-themed refrigerator magnets.

Homemade Coasters
A Quick Trick with Plastic Lids

Cool coasters make the perfect holiday gift!

Materials:
Plastic lids (several for each child)
Drawing paper
Crayons or markers
Clear contact paper
Scissors

Directions:
1. Collect plastic lids in the appropriate size for coasters.
2. Cut drawing paper into circles that fit the bottoms of the lids. (Children can do this themselves by tracing the lids onto paper and then cutting out the circles.)
3. Have each child draw a picture on one side of the circle.
4. Cover the drawings with clear contact paper and cut out.
5. Show the children how to trace a line of glue around the circle and glue their drawings to the lid.
6. Children can each make one coaster or several.

Notes:
• These coasters are for use with cold drinks!
• The perfect-sized lids can be found on round canisters of raisins.

Option:
• Instead of a drawing, have the children glue a photograph of themselves to the bottoms of the lids.

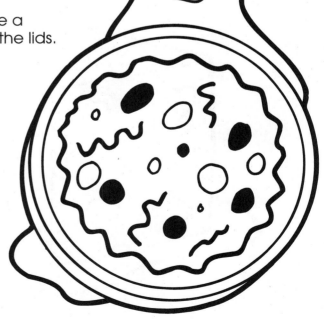

Unique Wrapping Paper
A Quick Trick with Cookie Cutters

Children can use this wrapping paper to wrap their own homemade holiday gifts.

Materials:
Plain wrapping paper (brown or white)
Tempera paint
Shallow tins for paint
Cookie cutters (stars, trees, gingerbread men, and so on)

Directions:
1. Give each child a sheet of wrapping paper.
2. Have the children decorate the paper by dipping the cookie cutters into the tempera paint, carefully shaking off the excess paint, and then printing onto the wrapping paper.
3. Once the paper dries, the children can use it to wrap presents.

Options:
• The paper itself makes a perfect holiday gift.
• Duplicate the Winter Holiday Patterns (p. 39) for the children to color, cut out, and glue to wrapping paper.

Holiday Scrapbook
A Quick Trick with a Manila Folder

This holiday scrapbook can hold cards or photographs.

Materials:
Manila folders (one per child)
Hole punch
Brads
Drawing paper
Crayons or markers

Directions:
1. Create a scrapbook for each child by placing several pieces of drawing paper inside a manila folder and punching two or three holes at the binding.
2. Fasten the pages into the book using brads.
3. Have the children decorate the front and back covers of their scrapbooks.

Option:
• Help children write their names on the covers of their books ("Devon's Holiday Scrapbook").

Holiday Sachets
A Quick Trick with Tissue Paper

This sweet-smelling sachet works to fragrance a drawer or to hang as an ornament.

Materials:
Tissue paper (in a variety of colors)
Pipe cleaners
Spices (cloves, cinnamon, nutmeg)
Yarn
Scissors (for adult use only)

Directions:
1. Cut the tissue paper into squares. Make one for each child.
2. Have the children put a handful of cloves or several sprinkles of other spices onto their tissue paper squares.
3. Demonstrate how to gather the ends of the tissue paper together and bind with a pipe cleaner. (Some children may need help.)
4. Add a loop of yarn to the pipe cleaner so that the sachet can be hung as an ornament.

Option:
• Add other spices to the sachets.

Pinching Picture Frame
A Quick Trick with Clothespins

Clothespins and clay come together to make unique picture holders, perfect gifts for family!

Materials:
Clothespins (spring-type, one per child)
Colorful modeling clay
Decorations (sequins, beads, glitter)
Glue
Photographs of the children

Directions:
1. Give each child a wooden clothespin to decorate.
2. Show the children how to make a ball with a small piece of modeling clay and then flatten it.
3. Have the children pinch their pictures with the clothespins, then stand the clothespin bases in the modeling clay.

Option:
• Instead of photos, the children can use the stands to hold small pictures that they've drawn.

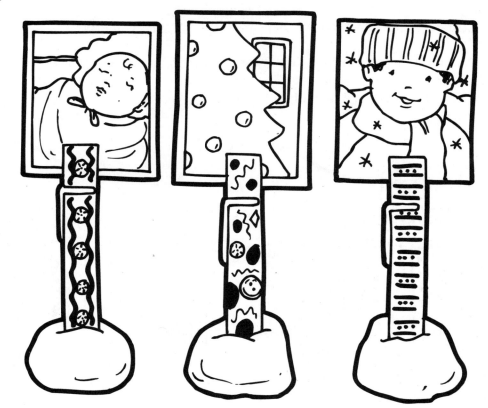

Miniature Gingerbread Houses
A Quick Trick with Milk Cartons

These gingerbread houses look good enough to eat!

Materials:
Small clean milk cartons (one per child)
Construction paper in a variety of colors
Scissors
Crayons and markers
Glue

Directions:
1. Give each child a milk carton. Explain that the children will be decorating the cartons to look like gingerbread houses.
2. Have the children draw pictures on the construction paper, cut out the pictures, and glue them to their houses. The pictures can be of candy, gingerbread men, and other treats.
3. Display the assorted houses in the classroom. Then let the children take them home.

Options:
• Ahead of time, trace holiday-themed cookie cutters onto construction paper and cut out. The children can glue paper gingerbread men, candy canes, and other decorations to the houses.
• Use the Winter Holiday Patterns (p. 39) for the children to color, cut out, and glue to their houses.
• Provide real goodies to glue to the houses, such as candy canes and gumdrops.

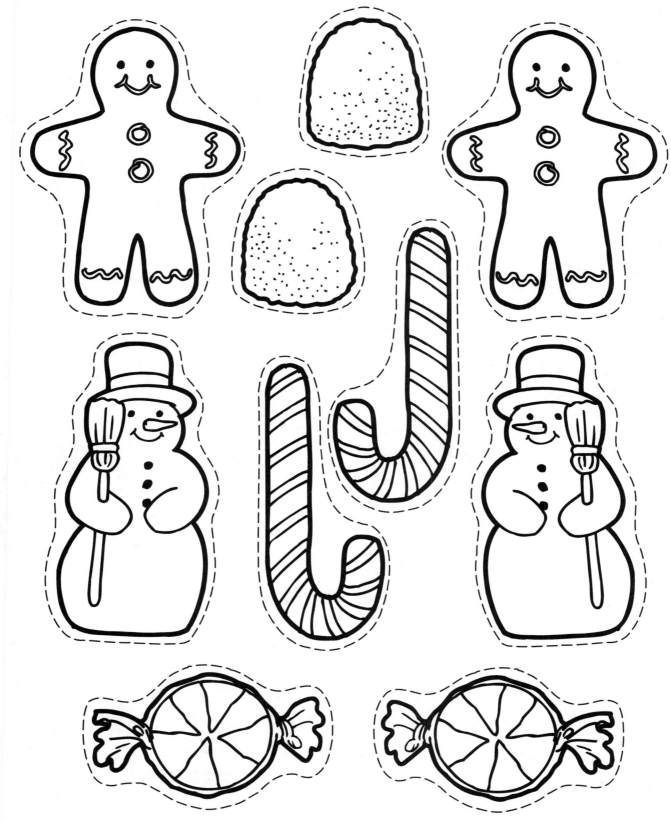

Personalized Ornaments
A Quick Trick with Photos

These festive and friendly ornaments can be used to decorate a tree, or they can be hung like pictures on a wall.

Materials:
Photographs (one per child)
Plastic lids (approximately the size that fits on a coffee can)
Glue
Decorations (sequins, beads, small buttons)
Hole punch
Yarn or ribbon
Scissors

Directions:
1. Have the children bring in photographs from home. (Explain to the parents that the pictures will be used in an art activity.)
2. Give each child a plastic lid. (Help the children find lids that will fit their pictures.)
3. Show the children how to trace the lids onto their pictures.
4. Help the children cut out their pictures.
5. The children then glue their pictures to the lids.
6. Provide a variety of decorative items for the children to use to decorate the rims of the lids.
7. Punch a hole at the top of each picture and thread through with a piece of yarn or ribbon for hanging.

Option:
• Instead of photos, the children can draw self-portraits for the ornaments.

Quick Tricks for Holidays ©2001 Monday Morning Books, Inc.

Hanging Picture Frames
A Quick Trick with Straws

Children can use these frames as holiday ornaments or gifts for friends or family.

Materials:
Drinking straws
Heavy paper
Glue
Ribbon
Photo of each child
Scissors
Glitter
Squeeze bottles

Directions:
1. Have the children bring in photographs from home. (Explain to the parents that the pictures will be used in an art activity.)
2. Have the children glue their pictures to the heavy paper and cut out.
3. Help the children to make frames around their pictures using the straws. They should cut the straws to fit around the pictures.
4. The children will then glue the straws in place.
5. Children can decorate the straw frames using glitter and glue.
6. Attach a ribbon loop to the top of each frame for easy hanging.

Options:
• Children can draw pictures to fit into their frames instead of using photographs.
• Children can bring in photos of family members or pets instead of pictures of themselves.

Decorative Candle Holders
A Quick Trick with Baby Food Jars

Create lovely votive candle holders from empty jars.

Materials:
Baby food jars (empty and clean, one per child)
Glue
Sequins, beads, and other small decorations
Tea candles

Directions:
1. Give each child a baby food jar to decorate using the sequins, beads, and other items. Have the children decorate the body of the bottles, staying away from the rim.
2. Insert a candle into each bottle.
3. Let the children take their candle holders home.

Note:
• Remind the children to never play with matches or light the candles on their own. These candle holders are for use only with adult supervision!

Jingle Bells
A Quick Trick with an Egg Carton

These music makers are perfect for the winter holiday season.

Materials:
Individual egg carton sections (one per child)
Small jingle bells
Glue
Scissors
Yarn
Decorations (foil, glitter, sequins, tinsel, tissue paper, construction paper, tempera paint and paintbrushes, and so on)

Directions:
1. Using scissors, punch a hole in the bottom of each egg carton section. Then give one section to each child.
2. Have the children use a variety of decorations to make their bell holders unique.
3. For each bell, thread a piece of yarn through the hole in the egg carton. Make knots on both sides of the hole, and tie a bell to the dangling yarn. (The carton section will dangle upside down.)
4. Teach children the song "Jingle Bells." They can shake their own jingle bells during the chorus.

Option:
• Children can make several of these bells and bunch them together.

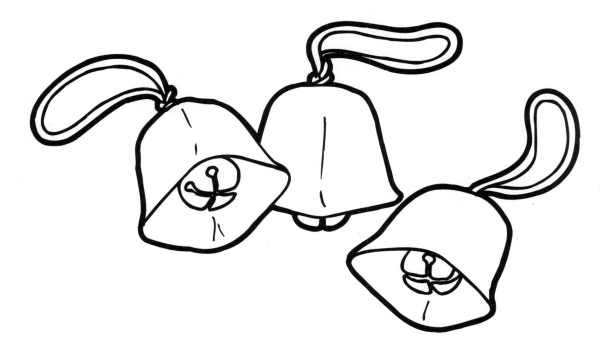

January: New Year's Day

January starts the year.
The weather's cold, winter is here.
February brings folks together.
And a groundhog tells the weather.
March is a time to wear your green,
And leprechauns are sometimes seen.

In April there is one main rule—
When playing tricks, shout, "April Fool!"
May is filled with springtime flowers,
Brought about by April's showers.
June brings the summer sun.
A time of fun for everyone.

Look out your window in July
When fireworks light up the sky.
In August drink some lemonade
While in a hammock in the shade.
September breezes shake the trees,
And out fall autumn's golden leaves.

October is a month that's dandy—
On Halloween collect some candy!
November bring your appetite,
To eat and eat Thanksgiving night.
December can be white with snow,
A winter's dream wherever you go.
The months fly by. The year is done.
Again, it's January one.

 Quick Tricks for Holidays ©2001 Monday Morning Books, Inc.

New Year's Eve Shaker
A Quick Trick with Paper Towel Tubes

Everyone likes to make noise on New Year's Eve!

Materials:
Paper towel tubes (one per child)
Tissue paper
Uncooked beans (or small items that rattle)
Glue
Nut cups (two per child)
Glitter

Directions:
1. Give each child a paper tube and two nut cups.
2. Have the children glue one nut cup to one end of the tube, sealing it shut. Let dry.
3. Give each child a handful of dried beans to pour into the tube.
4. Children use the other nut cup to seal the shakers closed.
5. Have the children decorate their tubes with tissue paper and glitter mixed with glue.

Options:
• The children can paint the tubes using tempera paint.
• Provide colored paper scraps to glue to the tubes.

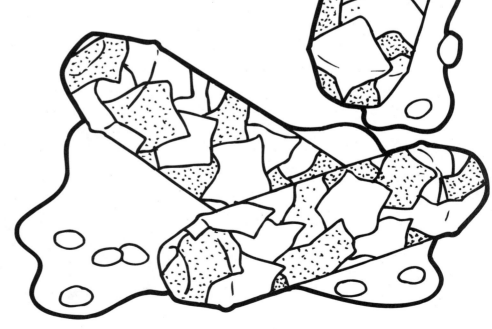

New Year's Eve Party Hats
A Quick Trick with Feathers

These festive hats will put children in the mood to celebrate!

Materials:
Construction paper
Scissors
Glue or paste
Tape
Tissue paper
Feathers and other decorations (ribbons, yarn, buttons)

Directions:
1. Cut the construction paper into strips. The strips should be about 12 inches (30 cm) long and 1 inch (2.5 cm) wide. Make three strips per child.
2. For each hat, tape two of the strips together at one end. Then fit the band around the child's head and tape the ends together to make a headband.
3. Tape the third strip of paper over the headband from one side to the other to reinforce it.
4. Have the children decorate their headbands with feathers, ribbon, and other creative additions. Then have a dress-up party and let the children wear their hats!

Option:
• The children can add pictures cut from magazines to their headbands.

New Year's Day Noisemakers
A Quick Trick with Paper Cups

Children will be able to shake, rattle, and roll on New Year's Day!

Materials:
Lightweight cardboard
Scissors (for adult use only)
Paper cups (one per child)
Glue
Plastic spoons (one per child)
Uncooked beans, macaroni, or pebbles
Decorations (tissue paper, glitter, construction paper, ribbon)

Directions:
1. Cut the lightweight cardboard into squares that will cover the open end of the cups. Make a hole in the center of each square just big enough for the spoon handle to fit through. Make one square per child.
2. Give each child a paper cup to decorate using the variety of materials. Let the cups dry.
3. Have the children place a handful of beans or other noisemaking items in their cups.
4. Have the children each slide a spoon handle through the hole in the cardboard, and glue the spoon handles in place. (They can add a piece of crumpled tissue paper to the hole if the hole is too big.)
5. Demonstrate how to glue the cardboard square to the cup with the handle sticking out. Let the glue dry.
6. The children can hold their shakers by the handles and make some noise!

Option:
• Children can cut items from old calendars to glue to the outside of the shakers. Or use the New Year's Patterns.

New Year's Patterns

Quick Tricks for Holidays ©2001 Monday Morning Books, Inc.

New Year's Pictures
A Quick Trick with Old Calendars

These pretty pictures can be hung on the wall in the classroom or sent home with the children.

Materials:
Glue
Glitter
Squeeze bottles
Calendars with pictures
Construction paper
Scissors

Directions:
1. Mix different colors of glitter with glue and place in squeeze bottles.
2. Remove the pictures from the calendars and place them where the children can see them.
3. Let the children choose one picture each.
4. Have the children decorate the pictures by tracing over them with the glitter mixed with glue.
5. Demonstrate how to make picture frames by cutting out the center of the construction paper and gluing it over the picture. (Help children who need it.)
6. Children can further decorate the frames with glitter and glue.

Option:
• Punch holes in the edges of the pictures and thread through with yarn for easy hanging.
(Holes can be strengthened with reinforcers.)

New Year's Dragon Costume
A Quick Trick with Cardboard Boxes

This cooperative costume is perfect for a Chinese New Year's parade.

Materials:
Cardboard boxes (big enough to fit over a child's head and torso; one per child)
Larger cardboard box (for teacher use)
Tempera paint
Paintbrushes
Craft knife (for adult use only)

Directions:
1. Give each child a cardboard box. Cut eye holes (or slits for eyes) at the appropriate level for each child. Armholes can also be made.
2. Work as a class to design the dragon. The children will each be one segment of the dragon's body. Decide whether all of the boxes should be painted with the same colors and patterns.
3. Have the children paint and decorate the boxes for the body of the dragon.
4. Create a dragon face on the large box and cut eye holes for yourself.
5. Stage a parade in the classroom or for the rest of the school.

Options:
• The children can further decorate the dragon with construction paper cutouts.
• This activity can be done with large paper grocery bags instead of boxes.

Quick Tricks for Holidays ©2001 Monday Morning Books, Inc.

February: Groundhog Day & Valentine's Day

Groundhog Day
On February second,
Go get your friends together,
Find a little groundhog
And watch him tell the weather.

If he sees his shadow,
Then winter snows will stay.
But if he doesn't see it—
Then spring is on its way.

*****

Valentine's Day
Valentine's Day means doilies and lace,
And cards that bring smiles to everyone's face.
So look out for Cupid, because it's his joy
To send arrows of love to each girl and boy.

Valentine's Display
A Quick Trick with a Clothesline

Decorate the room for Valentine's Day with this easy trick.

Materials:
Clothesline
Construction paper (red, pink, and white)
Scissors
Clothespins (spring-type)

Directions:
1. Cut out a variety of hearts. Make them different sizes and colors.
2. String a clothesline across the classroom.
3. Hang the hearts from the clothesline.

Options:
• Write a child's name on each heart. These could be your Valentine to the children.
• Let the children decorate hearts to hang in the classroom.
• Add cupids, doilies, and other Valentine's decorations to the line.

Quick Tricks for Holidays ©2001 Monday Morning Books, Inc.

Valentine Pouches
A Quick Trick with a Mailing Envelope

Children can carry their Valentines to and from school in these decorated pouches.

Materials:
Manila envelopes (one per child)
Hole punch
Ribbon or yarn
Scissors
Doilies
Glue
Crayons or markers

Directions:
1. Give each child an envelope to decorate using doilies, crayons, and markers.
2. Help the children to punch two holes in the top of the envelope.
3. Give each child one piece of yarn to lace through the holes.
4. Tie knots in the ends of the yarn to fasten the handle to the pouch.

Option:
• You can also use manila folders. Help the children to punch holes in the sides of the folders. Give each child two pieces of yarn to lace through the holes. Tie the two pieces of yarn together to make a handle.

Valentine Mailboxes
A Quick Trick with a Cereal Box

Children can slip their Valentines into these "mailboxes."

Materials:
Cereal boxes (one per child)
Construction paper
Glue
Scissors (for adult use only)

Directions:
1. Have the children decorate their cereal boxes to look like mailboxes.
2. Make a horizontal slit in each box.
3. When it's time to pass out Valentines, the children will slip them into each other's mailboxes. To empty the boxes, the children open the flaps on top.

Option:
• Children can decorate the boxes with additional decorations, such as doilies and glitter.

Cork-Printed Cards
A Quick Trick with Corks

Children can print interesting designs on their Valentines cards.

Materials:
Corks
Tempera paint
Construction paper
Heavy paper
Markers
Glue
Scissors

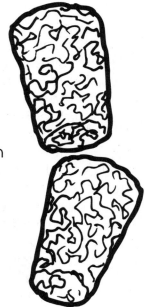

Directions:
1. Cut the heavy paper into heart-shaped templates. Make one per child.
2. Demonstrate how to fold the construction paper to make cards. Children can either fold the paper in half, or they can fold it in half and then in half again.
3. Have the children cork-print designs on plain sheets of construction paper using a variety of Valentine colors (red, pink, and white).
4. Once the paint dries, the children can use the heart templates to trace hearts onto their printed pictures. Help the children cut out the hearts and glue them to their cards.

Options:
• Children can decorate the cards with other items, such as beads or sequins.
• Children can print with other items.

Foil Hearts
A Quick Trick with Aluminum Foil

These silvery hearts are beautiful Valentines.

Materials:
Aluminum foil
Construction paper
Glue
Scissors
Crayons or markers
Heavy paper

Directions:
1. Cut out heart templates for the children to use. You can use the Heart Patterns (p. 57), or simply trace half a heart on a folded piece of heavy paper and cut out. Make enough for the children to share.
2. Give each child a sheet of construction paper to fold in half.
3. Have the children slip the heart templates on the fold of their cards and trace around the half of the heart. (The heart will be folded around the fold of the paper, so only half of the heart shows.)
4. The children cut out the hearts on the fold. When they open the papers, there will be a complete cut-out heart in the middle.
5. Give each child a piece of foil to glue to one side of his or her paper, covering the hole where the heart was cut out.
6. The children can decorate the paper around the foil heart and then present the Valentines to their friends or family.

Option:
• Children can decorate the cards with other items, such as beads or sequins.

Heart Patterns

Sweet-Smelling Valentine
A Quick Trick with Jell-O

This activity creates cards that smell as good as they look!

Materials:
Several boxes of red Jell-O (cherry, raspberry, or strawberry)
Water
Construction paper
Paintbrushes
Shallow tins
Resealable plastic bags (one per child)

Directions:
1. Mix the Jell-O with enough water to form a thick paste. Put it in tins for children to share.
2. Give each child a sheet of construction paper.
3. Have the children paint hearts on the paper with the Jell-O paste.
4. Let the Valentines dry. (This may take overnight.)
5. The children can give their fragrant Valentines to their friends or family. (For storage, they can put them in the bags.)

Option:
• Cover the Valentines with a sheet of clear contact paper or with plastic wrap to keep the Jell-O in place.

Broken-Hearted Valentine
A Quick Trick with Construction Paper

These puzzles are as fun to make as they are to put together.

Materials:
Construction paper (red, pink, white)
Glue
Scissors
Crayons or markers
Envelopes (one per child)
Heart templates for children to trace (optional)

Directions:
1. Have the children glue two different-colored sheets of construction paper together. For instance, they might glue a sheet of pink to a sheet of white.
2. Have the children wait for the glue to dry.
3. Demonstrate how to fold the glued paper in half. Then have the children trace or draw half a heart using the crease of the paper for one straight edge.
4. The children cut around the outline and open up the heart. They should have a valentine with a different color on each side.
5. The children cut their paper hearts into four large pieces.
6. Have the children challenge each other to put the hearts together again. (The puzzles can be stored in the envelopes.)

Option:
• Use the remaining heart borders from the cut-out hearts in another art project.

Valentine Doily
A Quick Trick with Doilies

This is a simple way to create pretty, frilly Valentines.

Materials:
Doilies (one per child)
Markers
Pipe cleaners
Glue
Construction paper

Directions:
1. Give each child a pipe cleaner and demonstrate how to bend a pipe cleaner into a simple heart shape.
2. Have the children create pipe cleaner hearts and then glue the hearts to doilies.
3. The children can color in the hearts with markers.
4. Let the children choose from assorted colors of construction paper to use for backgrounds. They can glue their doily hearts to the paper.

Option:
• Children can glue straws to the back of the doily hearts to create Valentine's Day wands.

Valentine Puppets
A Quick Trick with a Deck of Cards

This is a great use for a deck of cards that is no longer full! You only need the cards from the suit of hearts.

Materials:
Suit of hearts playing cards
Craft sticks
Glue
Queen of Hearts rhyme

Directions:
1. Glue a craft stick to the back of each of the cards.
2. Pass the cards to the children.
3. Teach the children the Queen of Hearts Mother Goose rhyme. The children can hold up the cards whenever their character is mentioned in the rhyme. (The number hearts represent the tarts. The "knave" is the Jack.)
4. Read the rhyme several times so that all of the children can have a chance to hold a card.
5. Store the cards and rhyme in a place where the children can reenact the story on their own.

Queen of Hearts
The queen of hearts, she baked some tarts,
All on a summer's day.
The knave of hearts, he stole the tarts
And took them clean away.
The king of hearts called for the tarts,
And yelled 'til he was sore.
The knave of hearts brought back the tarts
And vowed he'd steal no more.

Groundhog Puppets
A Quick Trick with Socks

Children can pretend to tell the weather while playing with their groundhog puppets.

Materials:
Socks (one per child)
Felt
Scissors (for adult use only)
Glue

Directions:
1. Cut the felt into circles for eyes, triangles for noses, and little ovals for tongues. (Use different colors of felt.) Make enough features for each child.
2. Give each child a sock. Have the children put the socks on their hands and glue the features in place.
3. Once the socks dry, the children can act out puppet shows with their groundhogs. They can tell the weather for the day!

Options:
• Children can draw on features using nontoxic markers.
• Older children can cut out felt features themselves.

Eyes

Nose

Tongue

Quick Tricks for Holidays ©2001 Monday Morning Books, Inc.

March: St. Patrick's Day

Today's the day to be seen,
Wearing something that's green.

Then search on every lawn,
For a small leprechaun.

He can be young or old,
But he'll lead you to gold.

Otherwise, try your luck,
To find something to pluck,

Search the whole green lawn over,
For a bright four-leaf clover!

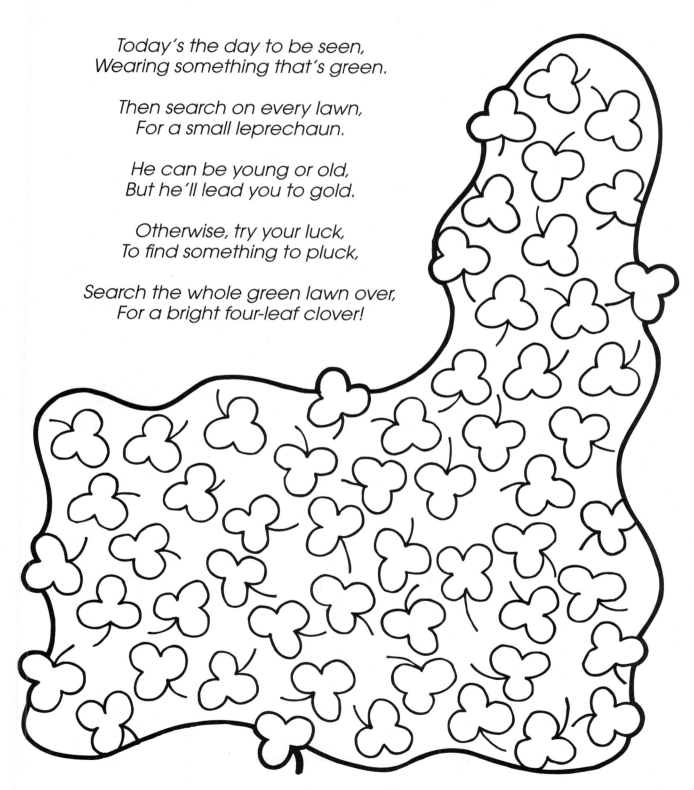

Pot of Gold Display
A Quick Trick with a Potato

Children can help make pot of gold displays for St. Patrick's Day.

Materials:
Potatoes (one for every two children)
Knife (for adult use only)
Gold (or yellow) tempera paint
Shallow tins (for paint)
Construction paper
Crayons or markers

Directions:
1. Give each child a sheet of construction paper.
2. Demonstrate how to draw an empty pot on the paper.
3. Cut each potato in half, and give one half to each child.
4. Have the children dip their potato halves in the paint and then use the potatoes to fill their pots with "gold" coins.
5. Post the completed pictures on a St. Patrick's Day bulletin board.

Options:
• Create a green crepe-paper border around the pots.
• Post leprechauns near the pots of gold.

Finding a Rainbow
A Quick Trick with a Mirror

This science experiment will help children find a rainbow on the ceiling of your classroom. But they might not find a pot of gold.

Materials:
Mirror
Pan of water

Directions:
1. When the sun is low in the sky and shining through a window, place a shallow dish of water in the sunlight.
2. Put a mirror in the water so that it faces the sun.
3. As the water "bends" the sunlight, a rainbow will appear on the ceiling.

Options:
• Have the children draw pictures of the rainbow.
• Discuss the order of colors that make up a rainbow: red, orange, yellow, green, blue, indigo, and violet (purple).

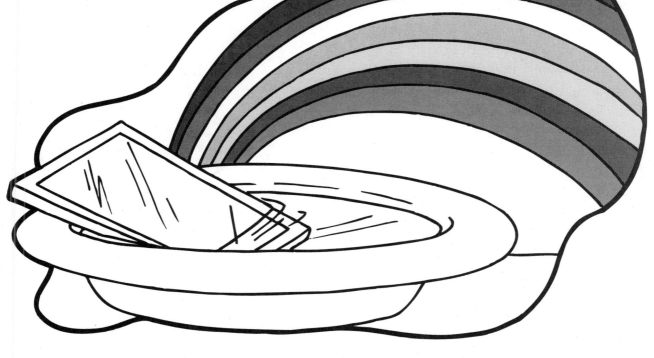

Green Clover Medallions
A Quick Trick with Ink Pads

These medallions will make sure that every child has something green to wear on St. Patrick's Day!

Materials:
Green ink pads (nontoxic, washable)
Clear contact paper
Construction paper
Hole punch
Green ribbon
Scissors (for adult use only)

Directions:
1. Cut the construction paper into small, medallion-sized circles.
2. Give each child a construction paper circle. Provide enough ink pads for the children to share.
3. Demonstrate this activity for the children. To create four-leaf clovers, they will dip their pinkie into the ink pad and then make four pinkie prints on the construction paper circles.
4. Punch a hole in each circle.
5. Help the children thread a length of green ribbon through the hole punch. Tie to form a necklace.

Option:
• Use green fingerpaint instead of ink pads.

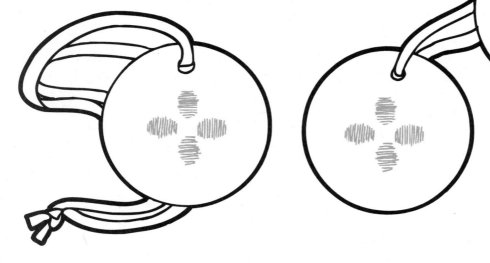

Quick Tricks for Holidays ©2001 Monday Morning Books, Inc.

St. Patrick's Day Rainbows
A Quick Trick with Straws

Seven children will work together to make rainbow paintings.

Materials:
Drinking straws (one per child)
Watercolor in rainbow hues (red, orange, yellow, green, blue, indigo, and violet)
Large sheets of paper

Directions:
1. Divide the children into teams of seven. Give each group a piece of paper, seven straws, and access to the rainbow of watercolors.
2. Explain that the children will be making rainbows. Each child will paint with one color. Help the children to organize themselves into rainbow order (see above).
3. Demonstrate how to straw paint. The children will place a blob of paint on the paper and then blow the paint with the straw. The first child should use red. Then have children add orange, yellow, green, blue, indigo, and violet. The paints will run together to create varied pictures and unusual rainbows.

Option:
• Post the completed, dry pictures in the classroom.

St. Patrick's Day Shamrock Wand
Another Quick Trick with Straws

These wands are perfect for use in dramatic play. Children can pretend to be leprechauns, pointing to the pots of gold.

Materials:
Drinking straws (one per child)
Green construction paper
Plastic lids (approximately 3 inches/7 cm in diameter; one per child)
Scissors
Glue
Crayons

Directions:
1. Give each child a sheet of construction paper and a plastic lid.
2. Have the children each draw four circles on the green construction paper by tracing around the lids.
3. The children cut out the circles and then glue overlapping sections of the circles together to form a four-leaf clover shape.
4. Demonstrate how to glue the straw to the back of the clover.
5. Let the wands dry before the children play with them.

Options:
• Children can decorate the clovers with glitter, beads, or sequins.
• Use the four-leaf clover patterns (p. 69).

April: April Fools' Day

There is one special time of year,
To play tricks on those you hold dear.

Not Halloween, or Mother's Day.
Not New Year's, or the fifth of May.

It's April first, yes, that's the date.
For pranks and tricks that are first rate.

Out of a can, out jumps a snake,
But anyone can see it's fake!

A flower that doesn't smell fantastic,
That's because it's made of plastic!

A card that opens on a spring,
An unexpected anything.

Just don't forget the one main rule,
When playing tricks, yell, "April Fool!"

Quick Tricks for Holidays ©2001 Monday Morning Books, Inc.

Puzzling April Fools' Cards
A Quick Trick with Holiday Cards

For April Fools' Day, children can make puzzles for each other using old holiday cards.

Materials:
Holiday cards
Scissors
Envelopes (one per child)
Clear contact paper or laminating machine (optional)

Directions:
1. Cut the cards in half and keep only the front parts (with the pictures).
2. Laminate the cards.
3. Let each child choose a picture, or pass out the pictures to the children.
4. Have the children cut the cards into several pieces.
5. The children can store the puzzle pieces in the envelopes.
6. Have the children trade puzzles and try to put the puzzles together.

Option:
• Photocopy the pictures before the children cut them apart. Have the children glue a copy of the picture to the envelope so they will know what the puzzle depicts.

Pop-Up Cards
A Quick Trick with Googly Eyes

For April Fools' Day cards, children can make things with springs.

Materials:
Googly eyes
Construction paper
Drawing paper
Glue
Crayons or markers
Scissors

Directions:
1. Cut pieces of construction paper into thin strips. Make one strip per child.
2. Have the children fold whole sheets of construction paper in half to make cards.
3. Demonstrate how to fold the thin strips of paper to form springs.
4. Have the children draw pictures on the outside of the cards.
5. Have the children draw small pictures on sheets of drawing paper and cut them out.
6. Demonstrate how to glue one end of the accordioned strips of paper inside the card.
7. Have the children glue the small pictures to the other end of the strips.
8. The children can glue the googly eyes to the small pictures.
9. The strips are folded up and the cards closed. When the cards are opened, the pictures pop up.

Option:
• Have children cut pictures from magazines instead of drawing their own.

Quick Tricks for Holidays ©2001 Monday Morning Books, Inc.

April Fools' Johnny Jump-Ups
A Quick Trick with Paper Cups

These little jack-in-the-cups are great April Fools' Day gifts.

Materials:
Styrofoam or paper cups (one per child)
Plastic spoons (one per child)
Paper nut cups (one per child)
Construction paper
Scissors
Glue
Crayons or markers
Tissue paper or yarn

Directions:
1. Give each child a nut cup to turn open-side down and draw a face on the bottom. They can add tissue paper or yarn hair. Let dry.
2. Have the children glue the round end of the plastic spoon to a wad of tissue paper and then glue the tissue paper inside the nut cup head.
3. Once the glue dries, make a hole in each child's cup and insert the spoon handle.
4. The children can make their little puppets jump up by pushing the spoon handles up and down.

Option:
• You can use individual egg carton sections in place of nut cups.

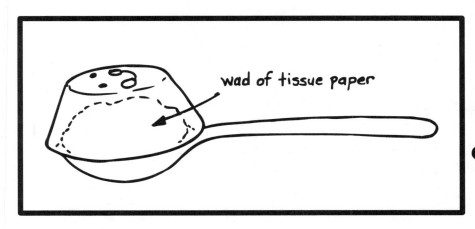

wad of tissue paper

Magic Pictures
A Quick Trick with Watercolors

These invisible drawings appear magically with an overlay of watercolors.

Materials:
White drawing paper
White crayons
Watercolors
Paintbrushes

Directions:
1. Give each child a piece of white paper. Have the children draw pictures on the paper with white crayons.
2. Have the children switch pictures with their friends. (Or pair the children up yourself.)
3. Provide watercolors for the children to use to paint over the pictures. The invisible drawings will suddenly appear like magic!

Option:
• Let the children paint over their own pictures.

Quick Tricks for Holidays ©2001 Monday Morning Books, Inc.

April Funnies
A Quick Trick with the Sunday Comics

These wacky creations will put the children's imagination to use!

Materials:
Comics from the Sunday newspaper
Construction paper
Glue
Scissors

Directions:
1. Have the children each cut out a number of different frames from different comic strips. (For example, a child might cut one frame from a cat-related comic and another from one about dogs.)
2. The children then organize the frames into stories and glue them to sheets of construction paper.
3. Once the picture stories dry, the children can trade their papers with friends and challenge them to decipher their wacky stories.

Option:
• Use black-and-white comics and have the children color them.

Earth Day Garden
A Quick Trick with Leftover Vegetables

Carrot tops will dazzle the students with new growth.

Materials:
Carrots with the stems and tops attached
Knife (for adult use only)
Shallow tin
Water
Small pebbles

Directions:
1. Cut the tops off the carrots leaving approximately 1 inch (2.5 cm) of stem.
2. Have the children fill the shallow tin with water. Add the small pebbles.
3. Arrange the carrot tops in the tin.
4. Place the tins in direct light.
5. During the week, keep the bottom of the carrots watered. New plant growth should appear within a week.

Option:
• Try this activity with beets.

City Gardens
A Quick Trick with Recycled Containers

Collect a variety of containers for this indoor garden.

Materials:
A variety of containers (margarine tubs, plastic cream cheese tubs, milk cartons cut in half, and so on; one per child)
Soil
Seeds
Instrument for poking holes (for adult use only)

Directions:
1. Poke several holes in the bottom of each container.
(This is for water drainage.)
2. Help the children fill their containers with soil.
3. Show the children how to make indents in the soil with their fingers for the seeds.
4. Give each child a handful of seeds to plant. Then have them cover the seeds lightly with soil.
5. Water the containers and place them in the sun. Monitor the plants daily!

Note:
Most herbs, such as parsley and dill, are easy to grow.

Options:
• Use seedlings instead of seeds.
• Have the children decorate the outside of their containers.
(These will then make perfect Mother's Day gifts!)

Leaf Prints
A Quick Trick with Leaves

Celebrate Earth Day with art made from nature.

Materials:
Leaves
Tempera paint
Shallow tins (for paint)
Construction paper
Scissors
Glue

Directions:
1. Take children on a nature walk to find leaves for these prints. Be sure to find them on the ground, not attached to a plant!
2. Give each child a sheet of construction paper.
3. Demonstrate how to make leaf prints by dipping a leaf, with the vein-side down, into a shallow tin of paint. Carefully print the leaf onto construction paper.
4. Children can make prints with one leaf or several. They can use more than one color of paint.
5. Help the children make borders for their pictures by cutting out rectangles of construction paper in a color different from the one used for the prints. Glue the borders to the picture.
6. Post the leaf prints in an Earth Day display.

Option:
• Use library books to identify the leaves so the children learn about plants and trees in their area!

Quick Tricks for Holidays ©2001 Monday Morning Books, Inc.

May: May Day &
Mother's Day

The flowers bloom, the birds all sing,
The leaves now have a bright green zing!
Oh, May's arrived, and with it spring.

We might just have a May parade,
Or sit and sip some lemonade.
On lazy days spent in the shade.

It's time for sunshine and blue skies.
For sunglasses to shield our eyes.
It's time to shoo off pesky flies.

And May is time to thank another
Someone special, yes, your mother!

Miniature Maypoles
A Quick Trick with Clay

Children can create miniature Maypoles to decorate the classroom.

Materials:
Drinking straws (one per child)
Clay
Ribbons (in assorted colors)
Glue
Paper plates (one per child)

Directions:
1. Describe a Maypole to the children.
2. Give each child a ball of clay to work into a ball and then flatten.
3. Have them glue the clay bases to paper plates.
4. Have the children each stick a straw into their clay bases.
5. Provide assorted ribbons for the children to glue to the top of the straws.

Option:
• Create a large Maypole in the classroom using long ribbons and a broom handle or other tall stick.

Quick Tricks for Holidays ©2001 Monday Morning Books, Inc.

Springtime Bouquets
A Quick Springtime Trick with Straws

Children can create colorful spring bouquets that never wilt.

Materials:
Drinking straws
Craft knife (for adult use only)
Stiff paper (oak tag or heavy construction paper)
Scissors
Crayons or markers

Directions:
1. Make a slit in one end of each straw.
2. Have the children create flowers on the heavy paper.
3. Help the children cut out their flowers.
4. Show the children how to slip the flowers into the slit end of the straws. The straws become the stems.
5. Children can make one or more flowers.

Options:
• Have the children decorate both sides of the flowers.
• Use glitter mixed with glue to add extra sparkle.
• Tie the bouquets with bits of ribbon in bows.

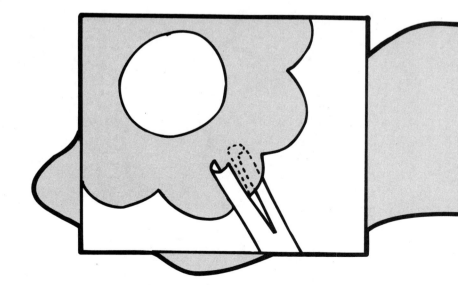

Doily Nosegays
A Quick Trick with Paper Doilies

These frilly decorations look lovely when captured with ribbon in a bouquet.

Materials:
Small doilies
Glue
Pipe cleaners
Ribbon

Directions:
1. Demonstrate how to form a doily into a flower shape. (Simply gather the middle and twist.) Then dip the bottom edge in glue and wrap a pipe cleaner around it. Or stick a pipe cleaner through the doily and twist to make a knot.
2. Give each child several doilies to make into flowers.
3. Help the children tie their doily flowers together with ribbons.

Options:
• Have the children decorate the edges of the doilies with glitter mixed with glue to add extra sparkle.

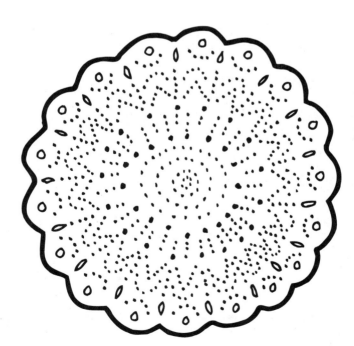

Pat the Bunny Pictures
A Quick Trick with Cotton Balls

Children can create their own miniature versions of the classic book *Pat the Bunny*.

Materials:
Cotton balls
Manila folders (one folder per child)
Hole punch
Scissors
Brads or ribbon
Crayons or markers
Drawing paper
Glue

Directions:
1. Cut a folder in half and then slide the halves together. Punch holes on the spine, add drawing paper, and bind with brads or ribbon. Make one of these books for each child.
2. Give the books to the children.
3. Have the children draw pictures on the pages. At least one picture should be of a bunny.
4. Provide cotton balls for the children to glue to their bunny pictures.

Option:
• Use colored cotton balls.

3-D Mother's Day Cards
A Quick Trick with Pipe Cleaners

These personalized cards will be cherished far more
than any store-bought ones!

Materials:
Green pipe cleaners
Photos of the children (or self-portraits)
Construction paper
Crayons or markers
Glue

Directions:
1. Demonstrate how to fold the construction paper into
cards. (Children can simply fold the paper in half, or fold
it in half and then in half again.)
2. Have the children draw pictures of flowers on the front
of the cards. They should leave a large circle in the
center of one flower.
3. Help the children to cut their photos (or self-portraits)
in circles to fit the center of the flowers.
4. The children glue their pictures to the flowers.
5. Have the children glue green pipe cleaner stems to
their flowers.
6. Ask the children to dictate messages to their mothers
and write them inside the cards.

Option:
• Cut a circle in the center of each card. Have the
children glue the full picture inside the card, so that their
face shows through the circle. The children draw a
flower on the front of the card around their face.

Quick Tricks for Holidays ©2001 Monday Morning Books, Inc.

Mother's Day Necklace
A Quick Trick with Junk Mail

This is one way to get rid of all those fliers that fill up your mailbox.

Materials:
Junk mail (colorful, glossy fliers work best)
Scissors
Glue
Yarn

Directions:
1. Show the children how to roll the fliers into thin tubes and glue the ends over. Wait for the tubes to dry.
2. Cut the tubes into sections to make the beads.
3. Have the children thread the beads onto necklace lengths of yarn.
4. Tie the ends together.
5. The children can take these necklaces home for Mother's Day gifts. (They also work well for grandmothers, aunts, sisters, and so on.)

Option:
• The beads can be painted with tempera paint.

June, July, August:
Summer

June, July, and August, too,
Bring playtime in the sun.
The light is bright, the days are warm,
It's time for lots of fun.

We celebrate some holidays with glee along the way.
There's Father's Day, and Flag Day, too,
And Independence Day!

So wave your flags and thank your dad
And have a good time, all.
Because all too soon school starts again
As summer turns to fall!

Quick Tricks for Holidays ©2001 Monday Morning Books, Inc.

Father's Day Pencil Holder
A Quick Trick with an Orange-Juice Can

Dads will be able to clear the clutter off their desks with these cool containers.

Materials:
Empty orange-juice (or other juice) can (one per child)
Glue
Fabric scraps
Scissors (for adult use only)
Heavy paper

Directions:
1. Cut the heavy paper into circles that are slightly bigger than the base of the cans. Make one circle per child.
2. Give each child an empty juice can.
3. Have the children decorate the cans with fabric scraps. They can make a collage of colors.
4. Once the glue has dried, the children can glue the bottoms of the cans to the heavy paper circles for bases.

Note:
This gift also works well for Mother's Day!

Option:
• Give each child one or two pencils to put in their pencil holders.

Father's Day Paper Clip Holder
A Quick Trick with Plastic Containers

These are the perfect holders for paper clips, staples, and other odds and ends.

Materials:
Empty plastic cream cheese tub with lid (one per child)
Construction paper
Glue
Crayons or markers
Scissors
Old magazines

Directions:
1. Give each child a clean, empty plastic tub.
2. Have the children either draw pictures or cut pictures from magazines to glue to the tub and lid.
3. Once the art has dried, the children can place the lids on the tubs and present this gift to their dads on Father's Day.

Options:
• Other plastic tubs work fine for this activity.
• Have the children dictate messages to their fathers. Place these notes inside the tubs.

Fourth of July Flag
A Quick Trick with Crayons

This patriotic activity is one way to use worn-down crayons.

Materials:
Red and blue crayons
Sharp knife (for adult use only)
White paper
Silver star stickers
Flag

Directions:
1. Peel the red crayons. Every child should have one.
2. Away from the children, cut V-shapes along the side of the peeled crayons. When children lay the crayons on their sides and draw across the paper, they will be able to make even lines.
3. Show the children the flag.
4. Have the children create the stripes of the flag using the red crayons.
5. Children can use the blue crayons and the star stickers to create the rest of the flag.
6. Post the flags in a Fourth of July display.

Option:
• Make flagpoles from wrapping paper or paper towel tubes and glue the flags to the poles.

3-D Fireworks Displays
A Quick Trick with Aluminum Foil

Use these glittering pictures in a Fourth of July classroom display.

Materials:
Aluminum foil
Glue
Colored construction paper
Crayons or markers

Directions:
1. Give each child a sheet of construction paper.
2. Have the children draw fireworks on their papers using crayons or markers.
3. Provide aluminum for the children to crumple or tear and glue to their drawings to add a three-dimensional feel to their fireworks pictures.
4. Decorate the classroom with the pictures.

Option:
• Strips of crepe paper can also be used with these pictures.

Quick Tricks for Holidays ©2001 Monday Morning Books, Inc.

Yankee Doodle Dandy's Hat
A Quick Trick with Macaroni

Post these patriotic pictures in a Fourth of July display.

Materials:
Construction paper
Uncooked macaroni
Feathers
Glue
Crayons

Directions:
1. Give each child a sheet of construction paper.
2. Demonstrate how to draw a hat shape on a sheet of construction paper. The hat can be a simple rectangle with a line under it for the brim.
3. Have the children glue macaroni all over their hats.
4. When the glue is dry, the children can glue a feather or two to the hat's brim.
5. Teach the children the Yankee Doodle song. When they reach the lines about Yankee Doodle sticking a feather in his cap and calling it macaroni, they can hold up their hats.

Yankee Doodle
*Yankee Doodle went to town
Riding on a pony
Stuck a feather in his cap
And called it macaroni.*

*Yankee Doodle keep it up.
Yankee Doodle Dandy.
Mind the music and the step
And with the girls be handy.*

Fourth of July Noisemakers
A Quick Trick with Paper Plates

These rattles will give the children something to shake on the Fourth of July.

Materials:
Paper plates (two per child)
Glue
Scissors
Silver stars
Crayons or markers
Uncooked beans, macaroni, or small pebbles
Decorations (glitter, construction paper, beads, sequins, yarn)

Directions:
1. Give each child two paper plates.
2. Have the children put a handful of uncooked beans, macaroni, or pebbles onto one plate.
3. Help the children to spread glue around the edges of both plates and press the plates together. They should hold the edges firmly for at least 20 seconds to set the glue.
4. Once the shakers dry, the children can decorate the plates. They can draw on flags, glue on silver stars, or create other patriotic designs.

Option:
• Make the shaker with aluminum pie plates instead of paper ones.

Summer Sand Painting
A Quick Trick with Sand

Powdered tempera paint transforms sand into a colorful medium.

Materials:
Sand
Jars with tight-fitting lids
Powdered tempera paint
Paper plates with deep rims (one per child)
Glue

Directions:
1. Create colored sand by mixing different colors of powdered tempera paint with sand in tightly sealed jars. Shake to coat the sand with the powdered paint.
2. Give each child a paper plate.
3. Have the children create sand paintings by drawing on their plate with glue and then adding the different colors of sand.

Option:
• Provide small seashells (or uncooked seashell macaroni) for the children to glue to their pictures for three-dimensional effects.

Summer Sand Art
Another Quick Trick with Sand

Children will love creating different pictures with colored sand.

Materials:
Sand
Jars with tight-fitting lids (such as baby food jars; one per child)
Powdered tempera paint

Directions:
1. Create colored sand by mixing different colors of powdered tempera paint with sand in tightly sealed jars. Shake to coat the sand with the powdered paint.
2. Give each child an empty jar.
3. Have the children create sand art by pouring layers of different colored sand into the jar until the jar is full.
4. Use glue on the insides of the lids to seal them.
5. Let the children take their sand art home to display.

Option:
• Turn this into a cooperative activity by having several children work with one jar. (You might use a bigger jar than a baby food container.) Each child chooses one color of sand to add.

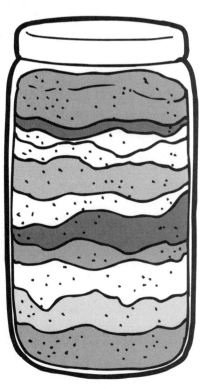

Quick Tricks for Holidays ©2001 Monday Morning Books, Inc.

Weather Puppets
A Quick Trick with Craft Sticks

Challenge the children to become weather forecasters with their craft stick puppets.

Materials:
Craft sticks
Colored paper
Crayons or markers
Scissors (for adult use only)
Glue

Directions:
1. Cut the paper into small squares.
2. On the paper squares, have the children draw pictures of different types of weather: sun (for sunny days), clouds, clouds with rain, and so on.
3. The children should glue the weather patterns to the craft sticks.
4. Each day, have the children observe the weather and then hold up the puppets that best demonstrate the weather outside.

Option:
• Duplicate the Summer Patterns for the children to color, cut out, and glue to craft sticks for this activity.